FAKE NEWS AND ALTERNATIVE FACTS

ALA Editions purchases fund advocacy, awareness, and accreditation programs for library professionals worldwide.

ALA Editions • **SPECIAL REPORTS**

FAKE NEWS AND ALTERNATIVE FACTS

INFORMATION LITERACY IN A POST-TRUTH ERA

NICOLE A. COOKE

Chicago 2018

© 2018 by the American Library Association

Extensive effort has gone into ensuring the reliability of the information in this book; however, the publisher makes no warranty, express or implied, with respect to the material contained herein.

ISBNs
978-0-8389-1636-0 (paper)
978-0-8389-1751-0 (PDF)
978-0-8389-1750-3 (ePub)
978-0-8389-1752-7 (Kindle)

Library of Congress Cataloging-in-Publication Data
Names: Cooke, Nicole A., author.
Title: Fake news and alternative facts : information literacy in a post-truth
   era / Nicole A. Cooke.
Description: Chicago : ALA Editions, an imprint of the American Library
   Association, 2018. | Series: ALA special report | Includes bibliographical
   references and index.
Identifiers: LCCN 2018009348| ISBN 9780838916360 (paperback : alk. paper) |
   ISBN 9780838917503 (ePub) | ISBN 9780838917510 (PDF) | ISBN 9780838917527
   (Kindle)
Subjects: LCSH: Information literacy. | Information behavior. | Media
   literacy. | Fake news.
Classification: LCC ZA3075 .C675 2018 | DDC 306.4/2—dc23 LC record available at
   https://lccn.loc.gov/2018009348

Series cover design by Casey Bayer. Series text design in Palatino Linotype and Avenir by Karen Sheets de Gracia.

♾ This paper meets the requirements of ANSI/NISO Z39.48-1992
(Permanence of Paper).

Printed in the United States of America
22 21 20 19 18   5 4 3 2 1

CONTENTS

PREFACE

At the 2017 American Library Association (ALA) Annual Conference, 2016 presidential nominee Hillary Clinton addressed thousands of librarians and information professionals. Clinton praised librarians for being on the front lines working for the benefit of their communities, and in particular, for encouraging literacy, reading, and the development of "curious, brave, informed citizens." She also commended libraries for safeguarding the First Amendment and providing services and resources to immigrants and refugees. However, it was Clinton's assessment of librarianship's most urgent battle that garnered deafening cheers and an ovation. She said that librarians "have to be on the front lines of one of the most important fights we have ever faced in history in this country: the right to defend truth and reason, evidence and facts" (ABC News 2017). In this post-truth age librarians are more important than ever.

Fake, or fabricated, news is expressly disseminated for the sake of earning money from clicks and views, and it is also used to mislead and misinform. With astonishing speed, fake news goes viral without being vetted or confirmed. Even if such information is eventually retracted or disproved, the damage has already been done and the false information remains digitally archived. This scenario played out in real time, and in epic proportions, in the months leading up to the 2016 presidential election. Now, after the election, increasing attention is being paid to fake news. But fake news is not new, nor are its relatives: hoaxes, satire, algorithmic biases, lies, alternative facts (NBC News 2017), and propaganda. It just has an alarming new veneer.[1]

It is also true that librarians have been engaged, and been pioneers, in the business of teaching information literacy skills and promoting critical thinking for decades, but this work has, in light of recent events, taken on new meaning and relevance for the public. Now librarians are being called upon to use our information literacy skills to help debunk and decipher fake news. We have a prime opportunity to help our communities and constituents become critical and savvy information consumers, which in turn benefits our nation's democracy. Librarians combating fake news and strengthening the critical thinking skills of our patrons is what this report is all about. This report will address the renewed phenomenon of fake news and its related concepts and discuss how a knowledge of information behavior and critical information evaluation skills can aid in combating the effects of fake news.

NOTE

1. "Alternative facts" is a phrase used by U.S. Counselor to the President Kellyanne Conway during a *Meet the Press* interview on January 22, 2017. During the interview Conway attempted to defend and sugarcoat alleged lies told by President Trump and former press secretary Sean Spicer. *Meet the Press* host Chuck Todd responded to Conway by stating that "alternative facts aren't facts, they are falsehoods."

INTRODUCTION

Read the following headlines and determine if the statements are true or false.

True or False? Ariana Grande Left Bloodied and Dazed after Manchester Bombing

True or False? Native American Names Deleted off Facebook

True or False? London Mayor Sadiq Khan Says Citizens Have No Reason to Be Alarmed Following Terror Attack

True or False? J. K. Rowling Mocks President Trump for Tweeting in the Third Person

True or False? Ireland Just Elected Their First Gay Prime Minister

True or False? Man Mowed Lawn during Tornado

True or False? Maxine Waters Blames the London Attack on Climate and Health Care "Inaction"

True or False? Fish Swim in the Streets of Miami at High Tide

- Why do these headlines ring true or false?
- If you saw these headlines on social media, would you share them with your networks? Why or why not?
- How would you present and explain these examples to others? What strategies and resources would you suggest?

See the "Revisiting the Headlines" section of this book's "Conclusion" for an explanation and discussion about these headlines.

FAKE NEWS IS OLD NEWS

A lie can run around the world before the truth has got its boots on.

—Quote often attributed to author Terry Pratchett, Winston Churchill, Mark Twain, James Watt, and various others

It's no secret that the Internet is saturated with information of all kinds, and much of the information is of low or no quality. Yet, before we can blink, this information makes the rounds without being confirmed. It is all too easy to believe the latest gossip or innuendo or get lost in YouTube videos featuring pets and pranks. Unfortunately, there is another, darker dimension of information found online—there is an excessive amount of web-based information that is both sensational and malicious, to the point of being harmful and even dangerous. Even if such information is corrected or disproved, the audience's attention has long shifted, the damage has already been done, and the original misinformation continues to float around online for future discovery.

It is now said that we live in a post-truth era—an era in which audiences are increasingly likely to believe information that appeals to their emotions and their personal beliefs, as opposed to seeking and accepting information that is regarded as factual and objective. People's information consumption is being increasingly guided by the affective, or emotional, dimension of their psyche, as opposed to the cognitive dimension. This post-truth reality is one of the reasons why fake news has become so inescapable, and consequently, why it's so hard to combat and interrupt the production and dissemination of deliberately false information.

The phenomenon of fake news is not new, nor is the concept of post-truth. *The Colbert Report* introduced us to the concept of "truthiness" over a decade ago, warning us, albeit comically, of the danger of accepting information and stories because they appeal to our emotions and not because they are supported by any real evidence or facts (Colbert 2005). Now, in 2018, journalists and the media remain on high alert and are warning their constituents about the "production of confusion" that surrounds the current presidential administration and encourages the industry that is fake news. Alternative facts are disseminated daily, and fact-based information or reporting that is negative or objected to is quickly and erroneously labeled as fake news, further obfuscating and suppressing information that citizens should be aware of and prioritizing.

THE NEED TO BE MULTI-LITERATE

In an age in which tweets and Facebook statuses are being reported as news, Internet users need to be competent and intelligent users of information; information consumers should be able and prepared to critique the "news" being broadcast, and they should be able to seek and find the information that is *not* being broadcast or otherwise prioritized. Additionally, they should be able to describe and understand the difference between the various providers and provocateurs of information. An approach to reaching this level of critical media consumption is to impart literacy skills to Internet users, many of whom patronize our libraries. Specifically, critical information literacy (Elmborg 2006; Eisenberg et al. 2004), digital literacy (Bawden 2008; Bawden and Robinson 2002), media literacy (Buckingham 2013; Hobbs 2011; De Abreu 2010), and ultimately metaliteracy (Jacobson and Mackey 2016, 2013; Mackey and Jacobson 2014, 2011; Witek and Grettano 2014) would facilitate the average user's ability to seek, find, and use appropriate and quality information, which in turn would facilitate more meaningful learning and understanding. Literacy skills would facilitate a shift from the routine crowd-sourcing of information on the Internet to the substantive evaluation and usage of information. Further discussion about metaliteracy and the importance of critical information skills appears in chapter 4 of this report.

Information creation and consumption will always be a significant part of our lives and our society, influencing how we understand and interact with the world. But the more information we have access to, the harder it becomes to pick out the good bits, use them, and relevantly apply them to our lives and individual needs. Formulating ways to educate users of all ages, inside and outside of formal educational and library settings, is an important topic that is not limited to any one area or group of people, or any one discipline of study. The procurement and implementation of literacy skills is a long-term and integral part of addressing the challenges involved in information consumption.

UNDERSTANDING THE CURRENT STATE OF THE MEDIA

Of particular note to this conversation is the role of journalism in the sphere of fake news. Jay Rosen, a media critic and professor of journalism at New York University (2017), warns against low-quality journalism and describes the "production of confusion" wrought in part by fake news and alternative facts by stating:

> The production of confusion is a method that the Trump White House is using as control, and the fact that when we're done listening to Kellyanne Conway, we know less as viewers doesn't seem to bother the journalists who interview her, and they're sort of slow in accommodating this fact.

The production of confusion is facilitated by the current administration's knowledge of the media's "deep grammar" and their subsequent manipulation of news outlets—they know that the media needs to have access to them, to interview them, to be privy to information and documents they are producing. Rosen suggests that this "deep grammar" of the media (the underlying and implicit business model of how the news outlets function) causes them to lower, or ignore, their standards and ethics, and not challenge fake news and alternative facts in the way they know that they could or should, because in doing so, they could inadvertently cut off their sources of information, rendering them noncompetitive (for example, when the *New York Times* is banned from White House press briefings, they are at a disadvantage when trying to analyze and report the news). Rosen further describes the "deep grammar" of the press by saying:

> The deep grammar is like the logic beneath the practice. So, for example, the fact that you need your interviewees to come back is part of the deep grammar of journalism, right? It affects a lot of what you do but it's not on the surface, it's not explained to viewers. It's not something that journalists would talk about very often. But certainly, Kellyanne Conway knows that and it gives her an advantage because she knows she has to be welcomed back.

But again, none of this is new. Journalism and media outlets are no strangers to controversy and manipulative tactics, nor are government or corporate entities unfamiliar with devices used to curry favor with, or penalize, journalists and the media. Consider the legacies of yellow journalism and propaganda and their particular relationships to political information and world events. Yellow journalism, synonymous with "the penny press," "jazz journalism," "tabloid TV," and "Internet gossip," is characterized by sensational or dramatic language and headlines, and exaggerated and potentially scandalous content that is poorly researched and often without merit (Cohen 2000, 8). Such stories are generated solely for attention and revenue (i.e., click-bait). Modern-day tabloids still engage in these practices, and social media is ripe with fantastic headlines and descriptions whose sole purpose is to get users to click and share. The goal is to employ "circulation-building gimmicks" that emphasize "drama over accuracy" (Cohen 2000, 18).

Propaganda is information of a prejudiced or disingenuous nature that is used to encourage a political cause or point of view (Stanley 2015). Propaganda utilizes the psychological devices of influencing and altering the attitude of a group toward a specific cause, position, or political agenda in an effort to form a consensus and to ensure a homogeneous viewpoint or belief. Propaganda is information that is subjective and is used primarily to influence the target audience and further an agenda, often by presenting facts selectively (perhaps lying by omission), or by using coded or suggestive messages or language to elicit an emotional response, as opposed to a rational response. Propaganda is often associated with material prepared by governments, but activist groups and corporate entities can also engage in propaganda. Despite its long historical context, propaganda is alive and well, and it has been at the heart of the criticism levied against Facebook after the 2016 U.S. presidential election (Shane and Goel 2017). Facebook at first denied any involvement in the dissemination of purchased advertisements designed to sway social media users, but it later admitted that fake Russian accounts purchased approximately $100,000 in targeted political ads prior to the election. The full effect of these ads is not yet known, but it has been established that these ads reached many people and may indeed have influenced their thinking and opinions, particularly if people did not realize that the information presented in the ads was fake. Propaganda is hiding in plain sight and influencing great multitudes of information consumers every day.

A cursory understanding of political economy and the underlying business structures of the news media is an important context for appreciating why fake news is so widespread and difficult to contest. More discussion about political economy, and the media's impact on information evaluation and consumption, is featured in chapter 3.

2
THE INFORMATION BEHAVIOR OF IT ALL

Information doesn't exist in a vacuum; rather, it is surrounded and shaped by context, both internal and external. In addition to the context produced by the financial and business dimensions of the media, the concepts of post-truth and truthiness also emphasize that there is a wide-ranging spectrum of motivations and emotions that motivate everyday information consumption. Information-seeking, information selection, information avoidance, and information usage (which are all part of the information behavior continuum) contribute to our understanding of how information is consumed on a daily basis, and provide further understanding of why consumers are susceptible to fake news.

LEARNING THEORY

A brief mention of learning theory is appropriate here in order to gain a meta-level understanding of how people acquire and absorb the information around them. The subsequent discussion of information behavior is informed by these larger concepts of learning and understanding.

In his work *The Three Dimensions of Learning* (2002), Knud Illeris positions learning at the intersection of internal and external cognitive, emotional, and social learning processes. Tapping into the fields of education, psychology, and management, Illeris posits that learning has two fundamental assumptions. First, learning involves two distinct processes: an internal psychological process in which new information is acquired and added to existing knowledge, and an external process in which the individual's information acquisition is shaped and influenced by their interactions with their environment. Second, the learning that occurs during these internal and external processes encompasses three socially situated contexts: the cognitive domain of knowledge acquisition, the psychological dimensions of emotion and motivation, and the social domains of communication and cooperation.

Similarly, Char Booth (2011), has written about reflective teaching and learning, and suggests that there are four factors of learning: memory, prior knowledge, environment, and motivation (42–46). When considering this typology, *memory* can be connected to the processing that one goes through when acquiring, filtering, and absorbing new information; information overload, which occurs when too much information is acquired and subsequently rejected, is also related to information processing. *Prior knowledge* refers to an individual's existing mental schemas and shapes the way in which new information is accepted or rejected; for example, mental schemas can be rigid and cause cognitive dissonance and reinforce confirmation bias and filter bubbles (more on this later in the chapter). An individual's prior knowledge can also indicate their readiness, or lack thereof, to receive new and/or conflicting information. The *environment* refers to the physical or mental factors that can influence information acquisition or rejection; for example, both anger and hunger could prevent an individual from being receptive to new information. The final factor, *motivation*, refers to the intrinsic and extrinsic factors that influence the procurement or dismissal of new information; an individual might be quite motivated to learn new facts when faced with an academic exam, and another person might be personally motivated to learn sign language to connect with a hearing-impaired friend.

What is important to note about the models presented by Booth and Illeris is that they emphasize the cognitive *and* the affective dimensions of learning and information acquisition. Learning, and consequently an individual's information behavior patterns, are complex, multifaceted, and dynamic. It is no wonder that the fake news phenomenon is so complicated and challenging to address and resist. The following sections will address two of the primary cognitive aspects, and then several of the affective aspects, of fake news.

MISINFORMATION/DISINFORMATION

The two cognitive dimensions of information behavior that are most applicable to fake news are misinformation and disinformation. Misinformation and disinformation (mis/dis) can be thought of as two sides of the same coin. Misinformation is simply information that is incomplete (Fox 1983; Losee 1997; Zhou and Zhang 2007), but it can also be defined as information that is uncertain, vague, or ambiguous. However, misinformation may still be "true, accurate, and informative depending on the context" (Karlova and Lee 2011, 3). The *Oxford English Dictionary* defines "disinformation" as "the dissemination of deliberately false information." This is especially true when the information in question is likely to be broadly and quickly disseminated, such as information on the Internet. Fallis (2009, 1–3) provides a more nuanced definition by suggesting that disinformation is carefully planned, can come from individuals or groups, can be circulated by entities other than the creators (i.e., misinformation spread by a news organization), and is typically written or verbal information. Hernon concurs by warning that "we can put quotation marks around anything and change meaning," and that mis/dis is so easily spread because "the person doing the misuse might only be guilty of making something publicly available, through a listserv or electronic journal or newsletter, without checking the original source" (1995, 136). The key to disinformation is that it is created with malicious or ill intent. However, it can also be motivated by benevolence (e.g., little white lies meant to spare hurt feelings, or lying about a surprise) (Rubin 2010; Walczyk et al. 2008). In such cases, it really is context that enables an individual to begin to make sense of the mis/dis (or information in general) being presented to them.

Because mis/dis is related to notions and discussions of credibility, trustworthiness, and deception, it can be hard to discern the motivations behind this type of erroneous information-sharing. These motivations are especially hard to discern in the online environment, where there is an abundance of information (both accurate and inaccurate) and often a lack of visual and aural clues, clues that in real life might alert a consumer of information that something is amiss or false. Because of the ubiquity of technology in today's world, it is particularly important to be conscious of mis/dis not only because it prohibits collective comprehension and intelligence, but because it can indeed do harm by prioritizing and upholding biased, misleading, or false agendas and opinions (i.e., propaganda). Zhou and Zhang (2007, 804) state: "with the growing use of Internet and ubiquitous information access, misinformation is pervasive on the Internet and disseminated though online communication media, which could lead to serious consequences for individuals, organizations, and/or the entire society at large."

AN EMOTIONAL DIMENSION OF INFORMATION BEHAVIOR

In addition to considering mis/dis as part of the information consumer's cognitive processing of fake news in the post-truth era, it is especially important to recognize the emotional, or affective, components of mis/dis; it is the affective dimension of learning and information behavior that enables us to understand how and why fake news has become so pervasive and hard to displace. One of the hallmarks of the post-truth era is the fact that consumers will deliberately pass over objective facts in favor of information that agrees with or confirms their existing beliefs, because they are emotionally invested in their current mental schemas or are emotionally attached to the people or organizations which the new information portrays. The affection dimension of information-seeking and usage circumvents the cognitive processes of information-gathering and selection. Among the examples of affective information behavior to be aware of are confirmation bias, filter bubbles (also known as an echo chamber), information overload, satisficing, and information avoidance.

It's easy for anyone, even information professionals, to become overwhelmed and overloaded by the sheer volume of information presented to us on any given day over the Internet and other forms of communication. Added to the sheer volume of information is information that is charged by political issues and involves potentially life-altering societal problems. The 2016 presidential election was such a time, no matter what a person's political party affiliation or leanings; information-seeking and use in such a fraught environment is stressful. The information behavior researchers

Donald Case and Lisa Given (2016) suggest that information-seekers during political campaigns may be "actively open to receiving new information and receiving it through serendipity, in an intense and condensed period of time" (30). Such information is often not as comprehensive or as rigorously vetted as one might prefer because the topics are so complex and "have such a wide range of opinions associated with them" (30). And "as the number of information items increases—or as the amount of available time decreases—people resort to simpler and less reliable rules for making choices to shorten their research time" (102). Contextually speaking, this information may also be impacted by personal experiences and viewpoints, and by a multitude of information sources "including news broadcasts, newspapers, magazines, the Internet, social media, and many personal conversations" (30) that may vary widely in regard to depth and clarity.

Social media plays a significant role in information overload because it facilitates the rapid dissemination of information, fake or otherwise. Instantaneously, stories can be shared, whether they have been read or not; for example, there is the accepted online shorthand of TL, DR—too long, didn't read—which gives people license to share and comment on content they've not actually read, much less evaluated (Gil 2016; Dictionary. com n.d.). The instant gratification associated with sharing online stories, "liking" something first, and collecting friends' reactions also encourages the dissemination of fake news.

Social media also encapsulates users into filter bubbles; filter bubbles (or echo chambers) are the result of the careful curation of social media feeds, which enables users to be surrounded by like-minded people and information that is aligned with their existing beliefs. Filter bubbles are further aggravated by confirmation bias, which suggests that users may actively seek and use information that already concurs with their existing mental models, prior knowledge, and memories, as opposed to seeking information from a variety of potentially conflicting sources. It is very easy for people to avoid distasteful, upsetting, or just incongruent information while in their social media filter bubbles. Filter bubbles are an example of selective exposure, or selective information-seeking, which is defined as the predisposition to "seek information that is congruent" with "prior knowledge, beliefs, and opinions, and to avoid exposure to information that conflicts with those internal states" (Case and Given 2016, 115).

Hand-in-hand with selective exposure is information avoidance. When purposeful choices are made regarding what information is obtained and consequently used, there are also purposeful decisions being made about what information is disregarded, evaded, or rejected in order to maintain existing states of belief (Case and Given 2016, 117). A final piece of the decision-making process, as it relates to information overload, selective exposure, and information avoidance, is satisficing. Satisficing is selecting information that is "good enough" to satisfy basic needs (36) or "choosing the first 'acceptable answer' to a question or solution to a problem" (102), "even if it means accepting a lower quality or quantity of information" (194). Satisficing could be a result of intellectual laziness, being unwilling or unable to deal with information overload, or not having the requisite information evaluation skills to reliably source information. Whatever the reason, satisficing also contributes to the spread and inescapabilty of misinformation, disinformation, and fake news by allowing low-quality information to remain in circulation and be disseminated; it may not be the best information, but it's "good enough" not to be questioned or challenged.

3

THE ILLUSION
OF INTERNET SAVVY

In conjunction with possibly detrimental misinformation and disinformation is the assumption that Internet users are savvy searchers and consumers of information because they are proficient with technological tools. Abercrombie and Longhurst (1998) refer to this as participation in "mediascapes"; mediascape participants are Internet users who are well versed in the mechanics of playing games, photoshopping, creating memes and mashups, and so on, but who aren't necessarily able to discern the information that is being manipulated and presented to them. Participation in mediascapes is a way for online users, especially younger adults, to communicate, interact, and be seen by their contemporaries. Use of the latest digital tools and media facilitates instant gratification and allows users to receive quick and widespread attention (Lankshear and Knobel 2011). The creation of memes, mashups, and photoshopped images is more about their producers and their "surface images, style, and brands associated with markers of identity and status" than it is about the content and subjects contained within these digital products (Abercrombie and Longhurst 1998, 82). Frequently, mediascapes involve celebrities or other public figures; these are images and personalities "that are often confused with the realities" and worlds of the people creating said digital products (Lankshear and Knobel 2011, 14).

POLITICAL ECONOMY AND THE ILLUSION OF CHOICE

Internet traffic, in the form of clicks and views, equates to revenue. Generating activity on a website to earn money is a driving force behind the creation and dissemination of fake news. There is a dimension of political economy that undergirds this era of online journalism and content production. Simply stated, *political economy* refers to the study of production (of a product), trade, and money earned from said production in trade. In many ways, the news media and journalism outlets engage in political economy—they produce a tangible product (a news report, whether in print, online, or in an audiovisual format) and they receive money for that product. To this end, it pays, literally, for a news source to be the first outlet to produce and disseminate a story, and to produce their product in quantity.[1] Fake news is now the newest version of this product, and in addition to an increase in quantity, there is a significant decrease in quality.

Once a rudimentary understanding of political economy is in hand, it becomes easier to identify the effects of political economy and recognize the influence that moneymaking has on our information consumption, particularly in and around social media. An amazing example of this hit the United States news in June 2017, when it was reported that there was a vending machine in Russia that allows users to purchase "likes" for their Instagram photos; for a price, and the alarming amount of uncertainty that accompanies providing a Russian vending machine with personal passwords and log-in information, customers can purchase hundreds of new followers and likes for their social media content.[2] Not only is this capitalism at its best (or worst), but it speaks to the deep-seated and compulsive need to be liked that manifests so clearly on social media, and has reshaped how people seek and share information—a need for instant gratification, a need for attention, and a need to further cultivate a filter bubble. Former Google product manager Tristan Harris says that consumers are addicted to social media and online content, which is exploited by online content developers, again, to earn online traffic and revenue. "Brain hacking," as it's called, capitalizes on information consumers' incessant need to check digital devices and see what new content has been posted, pushed, or highlighted online (Cooper 2017).

The Illusion of Choice

Holiday (2013) provides a fascinating account of how information is massaged, manipulated, and pushed up the media food chain where it receives buzz and high levels of attention and credibility, with little or no verification or validity. Most of what is considered mainstream, commercial, or traditional news and mass media comes from surprisingly few sources (*Columbia Journalism Review* 2017; Craft and Davis 2016, 87–96; Miller 2015, 315; Selyukh, Hollenhorst, and Park 2016; Vinton 2016). The highly concentrated nexus of media ownership revolves around a few large media conglomerates like Viacom, CBS Corporation, Time Warner, 21st Century Fox, Walt Disney Company, Hearst Corporation, and the Comcast Corporation (Le 2015; Pew Research 2017). The media oligopoly (the term used when a few companies dominate a market) also includes radio, print, and Internet holdings and venues that also produce and disseminate news. These entities also typically have blogs and other subsidiary sites attached to them.

Blogs, which the self-proclaimed media manipulator Ryan Holiday (2013) uses as a broad term to encompass social media and online information sources, need content, and a lot of it; they have no real news cycle like newspapers and television channels; rather, they need constant content in order to keep their followers engaged. "The site that covers the most stuff wins" (14). There is a certain power and cachet that comes with being covered by blogs and social media, and they need to maintain their reputations, even if these reputations are not based on providing high-quality information.

The economics of the Internet have created a twisted set of incentives that make traffic more important—and more profitable—than the truth. With the mass media—and today, mass culture—relying on the Web for the next big thing, this has created a set of incentives that have massive implications. The constraints of blogging create artificial content, which is made real and impacts the outcome of real-world events. Blogs need traffic, and being first drives traffic, so entire stories are created out of whole cloth to make that happen. This is just one facet of the economics of blogging, but it's a critical one. When we understand the logic that drives these business choices, those choices become predictable. And what is predictable can be anticipated, redirected, accelerated, or controlled—however you or I choose (Holiday 2013, 15–16).

THE RISE OF ITERATIVE JOURNALISM

The cycle of fake news begins with hyperlocal sites that have low or no barriers for information to enter the stream. Holiday describes the process of information, however questionable, being picked up by small blogs that seem to be monitored by the *Huffington Post* and other popular sites. Once that information is picked up, the "news story" is on its way. The key is to have knowledge of the right entry points that will facilitate the rise and spread of this fake, or partially fake, information. Similarly, there is legacy media, the "sister sites" of mainstream media outlets such as the blogs of newspapers and television stations. These sister sites benefit from the same branding, URL, and assumed quality of the main site. "Places like the *Wall Street Journal*, *Newsweek*, and CBS all have sister sites like SmartMoney.com, Mainstreet.com, BNet.com, and others that feature the companies' logos but have their own editorial standards [that are] not always as rigorous as their old media counterparts" (Holiday 2013, 21). Once information hits the sister sites, it is easier for it to reach national media platforms; these platforms need content and page views too, and are prone to look for and publish information that's trending and "bubbling up on the Internet" (23). The national media is taking the news at face value and is also not doing due diligence in regard to fact-checking or vetting information.

Subsequently, DJs, news anchors, and other "on-air" personalities now report on what they've seen and heard on blogs, YouTube, Twitter, and other social media platforms, instead of newspapers, television, and other more traditional sources of journalistic information. They are discovering and borrowing celebrity and gossip-based news that lacks credibility, but gains them viewers and listeners. They are engaging in what is referred to as *iterative journalism*—media personalities are reporting what they've heard, not what they have discovered or sought out directly. Their emphasis is on getting information first, whether it is right or wrong; false information can always be corrected later, even if no one sees or hears a correction or retraction (Holiday 2013, 167). The audience will have moved on by that point, with the false or inflated information still in hand. With iterative journalism, there is little distinction between truth and fiction, and there are no mistakes, just updates. This form of reporting is more about opinion and commentary than it is about the objective facts that journalism has traditionally been based upon.

This age of iterative journalism is due, in part, to three factors: the rejection of gatekeeping and control, "frustration with homogeneity," and the embracing of individual preferences. Added to this is the proliferation of online sources and information that seem to exist primarily on social media platforms. Holiday (2013) argues that our news media has become fragmented as a result (314–15).

Instead of the homogeneous news world of the past, in which most stories and reports essentially were the same, the fragmented news era boasts a heterogeneous news environment wherein accounts of one issue, topic, or event can differ significantly depending on the source. The proliferation of online news, particularly when mediated through social media or "micro media," provides niche content producers with a large number of platforms for targeted exposure to specific audiences. With a simple click of the mouse, change of the channel, or file download, consumers can choose a news media outlet that is most aligned with their ideological preferences. This is fragmentation in news. It provides more choice and possible exposure to wider perspectives in the news, though at the cost of a radical increase in the amount of biased or unbalanced reports propagating in the mass media (Holiday 2013, 315).

These high levels of personalization and preferences for heterogeneity, especially in online spaces, provide the perfect unmonitored environment in which fake news can grow and thrive.

The continual rise of blogs and the proliferation of information of all kinds represent a new era of information production, distribution, and consumption. In his book *Information 2.0*, Martin De Saulles (2015) discusses the explosion of citizen journalists; average individuals have so much access to technology that it is all too easy to capture pictures, audio, and video and upload them to Twitter, Facebook, YouTube, and any other online sites. These on-the-ground reporters are not only content consumers, they are also content producers, and they can publish this content themselves, or sell it to the highest bidder (e.g., the paparazzi). While some of this amateur-produced content is best described as gossip, some of this information is promoted as a means for social change and is viewed as a method of resistance and protest (e.g., videos of police shootings). Because there are low to no barriers for publishing citizen-produced content, it often circumvents vetting and traditional channels of dissemination. De Saulles refers to this as disintermediation (79). Technology changes the way information travels from its producers to its audiences. In most cases, these alternative pathways lead to "the disintermediation of traditional gatekeepers, including information professionals. Disintermediation is the bypassing of established players in a value chain either through the introduction of new technologies or via new business processes." Disintermediation is yet another reason why fake news thrives, because information can travel from content producer to consumer in a matter of seconds without being vetted by intermediaries such as reputable news organizations. And this lack of vetting or confirmation can be a disservice to the consumer, who may not be aware of the low quality of the information being consumed or may not have the skills to discern otherwise. So where does this leave information professionals, who for years have been teaching and promoting information literacy skills and education? We continue to do what we've always done, but we need to address the development of critical thinking skills with greater context. The cognitive and emotional dimensions of learning and information acquisition need to be considered, and in addition to teaching patrons and students how to evaluate information that is presented to them, we need to teach them how to think about the production of information and the back-end workings of their favorite information sources. Information professionals are increasingly tasked with teaching patrons to prepare for "critical analysis for responsible engagement" (Miller 2015, 315).

> There is a danger that users of these information services will be unaware of the filtering that is taking place and assume the information they are being presented with is representative of the broader universe of data that exists on the open web. So rather than simply showing users how to perform better searches, a role for many information professionals will be to help information seers better understand what is going on in the backend systems of Google, Facebook, Amazon, and other Internet services. (De Saulles 2015, 126)

Patrons need to know the "what" of the information they're consuming, and they also need to recognize and understand the "who," "why," "how," and "when" of information production, dissemination, and consumption. Librarians (along with educators and journalists) are now in the position of being "truth workers" in an age of "factual recession" (Head and Wihbey 2017), taking their information literacy skills, messages, and outreach to a whole new level.

NOTES

1. Fake news producers are keenly aware of the media's need to be first with a scoop, and they recognize that news outlets will run with a story even if it has not been completely vetted or confirmed. In July 2017, the television journalist Rachel Maddow claimed that she was sent fake National Security Administration documents; presumably the goal was to have Maddow run the story so a campaign could then be launched to attack her credibility, costing her viewers' trust (Borchers 2017). Fake news producers are in many cases savvier than the average media or news consumer, and they are proactively trying to undermine the people and venues that seek to expose them. The post-truth era is a precarious one.

2. B. Feldman, "In Russia, You Can Buy Instagram Likes from a Vending Machine," June 8, 2017, http://nymag.com/selectall/2017/06/you-can-buy-instagram-likes-from-a-russian-vending -machine.html; Y. Tan, "There's a Vending Machine Selling Fake Instagram Likes, Because This Is What We've Become," June 7, 2017, http://mashable.com/2017/06/07/instagram -likes-vending-machine/#QRODfQKZNmqa.

4

CRITICAL THINKING AND METALITERACY

Misinformation and disinformation in conjunction with the false illusion of Internet and media savvy are problematic in their own right. Combine this with post-truth, truthiness, filter bubbles, and confirmation bias, and it's no wonder that fake news is so widespread. In an age in which Tweets and Facebook statuses are being reported as news and likes and shares are more sought after than the truth, information consumers need to be knowledgeable, sharp, tireless, and active users and creators of information in order to actually discern facts and true statements. This level of critical media consumption requires an understanding of why consumers are especially susceptible to fake news. Then we need to impart literacy skills to these users. Information professionals are perfectly poised to accept this challenge of improving critical media consumption, and expand existing information literacy conversations, strategies, and techniques.

CRITICAL THINKING

> *Thinking is an action.*
> —bell hooks 2010, 7

In her writings about education and the need for improved and engaged pedagogy, the educator and writer bell hooks denounces the devaluation of the innate inquisitiveness and appetite that children have for learning; she argues that the interactive processes that young children employ to learn about their surroundings become passive once they begin formal schooling. Formal education teaches children to consume information without question in an effort "to educate them for conformity and obedience" (2010, 8). hooks challenges students and teachers to relish independent thoughts and reconnect with critical thinking. She says that critical thinking involves "discerning the who, what, when, where, and how of things—and then utilizing that knowledge in a manner that enables you to determine what matters most" (9).

There are other authors who, while taking a psychological or journalistic approach, concur with hooks and encourage information consumers to be proactive and selective with the information they absorb and act upon. Kovach and Rosenstiel (2011) suggest that consumers should be skeptical; this does not mean that individuals should be pessimistic and reject everything they hear and see. Rather, readers and listeners should not indiscriminately accept what they see and hear; instead, they should be continually questioning the information being presented, even if it's presented by a trusted source. The authors also suggest that the current information divide in our (post-truth) society is that between those who create information and content, and those who consume that information in an uncritical way. Jackson and Jamieson (2007) refer to this as being caught up in the spin. Spin, which is equivalent to misinformation and sometimes disinformation, "paints a false picture of reality by bending facts, mischaracterizing the words of others, ignoring or denying crucial evidence, or just 'spinning a yarn,' by making things up" (vii). Levitin (2016) concurs and refers to this as *counter knowledge*, which is "misinformation packaged to look like fact and that some critical mass of people has begun to believe" (168). Counter knowledge, like mis/dis, can thrive because it may indeed contain a kernel of truth, some level of believability, and social capital that make it believable (170).

Fake news, spin, and counter knowledge profit from "persuasion by association" (Levitin 2016, 176), which explains that when mis/dis comes from a reliable, and perhaps mostly ingenuous source, it is likely not to be detected or interrogated. A good example of this particular phenomenon is Brian Williams, the former anchor of NBC's *Nightly News*, who was terminated from his position for "embellishing" his reports and "misrepresenting" his participation in the stories he covered (Calamur 2015). Because Williams was considered a trusted source of information, his aggrandizements went undetected for years. Spin and counter knowledge are unquestionably precursors of fake news and alternative facts. Being curious, asking questions, respecting facts, and evaluating sources help information consumers to become "unspun," become critical consumers, and become resistant to the spin often presented in the media (179).

CRITICAL MEDIA CONSUMPTION THROUGH MULTIPLE LITERACY INSTRUCTION

There is no shortage of misinformation and disinformation on the Internet, and despite the rapid nature of their dissemination and their recalcitrant staying power, there are any number of sources that can be consulted to authenticate and repudiate suspect information. Snopes.com (www.snopes.com), the Centers for Disease Control (www.cdc .gov/hoax_rumors.html), Know Your Meme (http://knowyourmeme.com), and PolitiFact (www.politifact.com) are but a few examples of recognized sites that regularly address and debunk hoaxes, rumors, and urban legends that circulate on the Internet. Started in 1995, Snopes.com researches circulated stories and provides the historical context of rumors. The Centers for Disease Control (CDC) is a U.S. government agency, and its website is an easy way to confirm or deny medical information and rumors. Know Your Meme is another site that gives comprehensive information about the messages, visuals, and videos that appear regularly on social media sites. And PolitiFact is among the sites that deal specifically with political information and fodder. Since everyone has their own beliefs and opinions, all sites may not be appropriate for every audience; news sites, and the sites that aim to dispel myths, rumors, and other hoaxes, are variously categorized as liberal, conservative, left-leaning, right-leaning, or otherwise biased (Attkisson 2017; Jerz 2016). With this in mind, part of being a savvy consumer is being open to ideas that differ from your own, and locating sites that are appropriate yet still adhere to some basic tenets of information evaluation, such as referencing multiple sources to confirm information and checking sites for currency and reputable authors/creators. (Please see chapter 5 for more suggestions for evaluating information sources.)

In the days following the 2016 presidential election, numerous lists and sites emerged to shed light on the panoply of fake news, satire, propaganda, and otherwise misleading sites that currently dominate social media feeds, especially as it pertains to political information. Computer coders and hackers have joined the struggle, creating plug-ins that help Internet users understand dubious sites that appear in their news feeds and browsers; however, these hacks do not, and should not, take the place of individuals doing manual due diligence. Information evaluation cannot be totally outsourced. The majority of disinformation on the Internet could be uncovered with rudimentary evaluation skills. If information consumers would take the time and effort to make a few simple assessments, disinformation wouldn't be so prevalent or insidious. In order to become critical consumers of information, users should question the currency of the information (or lack thereof), carefully examine the site's URL, consider the language being used (i.e., language that is melodramatic, provocative, or absolute), consider the reasonableness of the information, and consider the reputation and leanings of the website providing the information (e.g., The Onion is a known satire site, and stories with that byline should be treated as fiction even if the headlines and content seem realistic). Another question to ask is if the information is reported elsewhere online (i.e., triangulating information). Although these are ostensibly easy questions to ask, critical information consumption is not instinctive and Internet users need to be taught to evaluate, organize, and effectively use information. Information consumers need to be proficient in multiple forms of literacy (Area and Pessoa 2012; Cope and Kalantzis 2009; New London Group 1996; Walsh 2010).

Specifically, critical information literacy (Eisenberg, Lowe, and Spitzer 2004; Elmborg 2006) and digital literacy (Bawden 2008; Bawden and Robinson 2002) would aid the average Internet user's ability to seek, find, and use quality information, which in turn would promote more thoughtful discourse and learning. Critical information consumers should be literate in multiple domains and able to apply quality information to their daily lives. Such literacy skills would facilitate a shift from routine and mindless information-sharing and acceptance to the substantive evaluation of information.

Information literacy[1] has long been discussed and taught in libraries, and refers to acquiring and building up the capacity to read, interpret, assess, and use information in everyday life (Kuhlthau 1987). Information literacy is not the same as conventional skills-based literacy; rather, it refers to a frame of reference for consuming information, or a type of critical thinking. Information literacy considers the larger context in which information is discovered and consumed, and it encourages users to seek information that is relevant and has the potential to be useful over the long term. Critical information literacy extends the concept of information literacy by advocating that information be viewed in situ, and that it be evaluated in relation to the underlying power structures that shape all information, and the acquisition of agency that comes with the acquisition of quality information (Accardi, Drabinski, and Kumbier 2010; Booth 2011; Elmborg 2006; Tisdell 2008).

Because the current proliferation of fake news is happening primarily online, digital literacy skills are also important to contemplate and incorporate. Along with the related concepts of media and visual literacy, digital literacy is in essence about being "deeply literate in the digital world" and being "skilled at deciphering complex images and sounds as well as the syntactical subtleties of words" (Lanham 1995). Paul Gilster (1997) describes digital literacy as the mastering of ideas and not keystrokes (or other techniques and technologies). The focus of media literacy is more specific, focusing on mass media such as television and radio, often when examining popular culture. Media literacy also examines media production, video games, and print products like comic books and graphic novels. Visual literacy (also referred to as graphic literacy) examines electronic and other types of visually based images, and focuses on the ability to decipher imagery and the intentional and unintentional messages that are projected therein.

Metaliteracy

While discrete areas of literacy are certainly important (e.g., media, digital, cyber, visual, mobile, health, new media, ICT, and information fluency), this report advocates that critical consumers of information adapt a metaliteracy approach. Thomas P. Mackey and Trudi E. Jacobson (2011, 2014) discuss metaliteracy as it pertains to library and information science. They describe metaliteracy in the following way:

> Metaliteracy is an overarching and self-referential framework that integrates emerging technologies and unifies multiple literacy types. This redefinition of information literacy expands the scope of generally understood information competencies and places a particular emphasis on producing and sharing information in participatory digital environments. (2011, 62–63)

Specifically, metaliteracy asks us to understand the format type and delivery mode of information; evaluate dynamic content critically; evaluate user feedback of information; produce original content in multiple media formats; create a context for user-generated information; understand personal privacy, information ethics, and intellectual property issues; and share information in participatory environments (Mackey and Jacobson

2011). Metaliteracy clearly encompasses standard elements of information and other literacies, but it challenges information professionals to take a step back and look at the bigger literacy picture. Metaliteracy encourages critical thinking and collaboration, particularly in an online environment, and encourages participants to be active in the construction and distribution of knowledge. Metaliteracy provides a holistic lens through which to contemplate how critical consumers can interact with information; this approach focuses on the individual consumer, and puts an equal emphasis on the context that shapes information production and consumption.

> The individual is a key part of the process, but the social context helps shape the experience. Social media environments are socially constructed spaces that rely on the contributions of individuals to create meaning. (Mackey and Jacobson 2014, 4)

Ultimately, the metaliterate learner is the active learner that bell hooks writes about (2010, 7). "The metaliterate learner is an active participant who is an effective communicator and translator of information. The metaliterate learner is an author of information in many forms" (Mackey and Jacobson 2014, 91). Metaliterate learners are critically engaged learners and are themselves content producers, who can contribute to discourse and can also successfully navigate the information landscape that is riddled with alternative facts, biases, spin, and counter knowledge. It is the metaliterate learner who may be the best equipped to confront and dispel fake news. Those in information professions, particularly the library profession, which has a long history of the practice and study of information literacy, are well positioned to work with the general public to improve critical thinking and information evaluation skills, and to promote the benefits of being metaliterate. Information professionals have a renewed opportunity and enhanced platform to assert their expertise and their willingness to co-create knowledge with their constituents.

NOTE

1. Please see the "Appendix: Additional Resources" later in this book for reading recommendations to engage more deeply with the literature surrounding the various forms of literacy.

5
CONCLUSION

"The era of the penny press, yellow journalism, and jazz journalism is still with us in a new format, but quite recognizable. It just hasn't been given a new name" (Cohen 2000, 121). Fake news is not new, it's just the latest moniker for an age-old phenomenon; and consequently, it's not going away. When the fake news moniker has faded, the problem will still exist, and eventually it will reemerge with a new name. While we are currently living in a post-truth era, information will continue to proliferate and dominate our society, coloring how we learn, play, and interact with the world. The more information we have access to, the harder it becomes to pick out the good bits, use them, and relevantly apply them to our lives. Devising ways to educate consumers of all ages, inside and outside of formal educational settings, is an important topic that is not limited to any one area or group of people, or any one discipline of study. The acquisition and implementation of metaliteracy skills are a long-term and integral part of addressing the reach and influence of fake news and misinformation and disinformation.

REVISITING THE HEADLINES

Let's return to the *True or False?* headlines from chapter 1.

> *True or False?* Ariana Grande Left Bloodied and Dazed after Manchester Bombing

> *False.* A picture of a seemingly bloodied Grande was circulated, primarily on Twitter, after the terrorist bombing that occurred outside of her May 2017 concert in Manchester, England. The picture was taken years earlier on the set of an American television show entitled *Scream Queens*, which was a comedic horror story. The picture of Grande was from the set, after the scene where her character was killed and she was wearing fake blood. While the events and the picture were real in their own rights, they were mashed together, yellow journalism-style, to create a more dramatic and click-worthy Internet story.

> *Check the source:* "Ariana Grande Emerges with Cut and Bloodied Face Following Scream Queens Filming," www.mirror.co.uk/3am/celebrity-news/ariana -grande-emerges-cut-bloodied-5940376

True or False? Native American Names Deleted off Facebook

True. There have been several occasions and stories about Native American social media users having their Facebook accounts suspended or deleted for using "fake names." Tribal names have erroneously been considered fake, and are either reported to Facebook by other users or flagged by Facebook staff. These users have had to produce identification with their legal names in order to restore their accounts. Some users have reported having their accounts suspended or deleted more than once.

Check the source: "Facebook Still Suspending Native Americans Over 'Real Name' Policy," https://www.theguardian.com/technology/2015/feb/16/facebook-real-name-policy-suspends-native-americans

True or False? London Mayor Sadiq Khan Says Citizens Have No Reason to Be Alarmed Following Terror Attack

True and False. After the May 2017 terrorist bombing in Manchester, England, London Mayor Sadiq Khan was criticized on social media for downplaying events and advising citizens not to be alarmed. In fact, Khan did express that sentiment, but his full statement reveals that he actually advised his constituents to not be alarmed by the increased police presence in the aftermath of the bombing. This is a prime example of comments taken out of context, and the lack of context can create confusion and completely change the meaning of the original remarks. It is not quite yellow journalism, but the effect is the same: salacious headlines that get people's attention for the wrong reasons.

Check the source: "London's Mayor Said There's 'No Reason to Be Alarmed' by a Terrorist Attack?" www.snopes.com/2017/06/04/london-mayor-sadiq-khan-no-reason-to-be-alarmed-trump

True or False? J. K. Rowling Mocks President Trump for Tweeting in the Third Person

True. While the headline may not seem true, it is indeed a factual statement. However ridiculous it may seem to people who do not follow *Harry Potter* author J. K. Rowling, she does indeed mock, or troll, Donald Trump on a regular basis on social media.

Check the source: "J. K. Rowling Mocks President Trump for Tweeting in the Third Person," http://time.com/4765203/j-k-rowling-donald-trump-third-person-tweet

True or False? Ireland Just Elected Their First Gay Prime Minister

True. In June 2017 Leo Varadkar was indeed elected Ireland's prime minister. While the headline is correct, the wording is reductionist and could be perceived as questionable to readers not familiar with Varadkar, Ireland, or the country's political climate. The wording of the headline is designed to entice clicks or views. Varadkar is indeed gay and he is of Indian descent; his election is a celebration of diversity and indicative of the strides that Ireland has made in recent years.

Check the source: "Leo Varadkar Was Just Voted to Become Prime Minister of Ireland," www.teenvogue.com/story/leo-varadkar-was-just-voted-prime-minister-of-ireland?mbid=social_facebook

True or False? Man Mowed Lawn during Tornado

True. In June 2017 a spectacular picture made the social media rounds, showing a man mowing his lawn with a large and significant funnel cloud in the background. The picture was initially thought to be fake, a photoshopped image created to get attention. This example draws attention to the proliferation of fake images that exist and are shared online. It's also an example that indicates that audiences do have some level of skepticism when consuming information and visual images.

Check the source: "Man Mowed Lawn during Tornado?" www.snopes.com/man-mowed-lawn-tornado/?utm_source=facebook&utm_medium=social

True or False? Maxine Waters Blames the London Attack on Climate and Health Care "Inaction"

False. After the May 2017 terrorist bombing in Manchester, England, it was reported that U.S. Congresswoman Maxine Waters made these claims about the cause of the British tragedy via Twitter. In fact, the tweet was sent from a parody account @MaxineVVaters (notice the two capital Vs designed to look like the W in Waters). The fake account copied Waters's profile picture and details to mimic her real account and look official to cursory glances. The congresswoman's actual Twitter account is @MaxineWaters and is verified with the platform's blue checkmark, which indicates that the account has been vetted and certified to be a legitimate account. This is an example of a fake account, which are very common, and reminds us to be wary of tweets that are reported in other venues, for example, tweets that are embedded in articles and other social media platforms. There are many fake tweet generators that mimic legitimate accounts, usually of celebrities and other public figures, and that are used to trick readers and spread disinformation. Examples of tweet generators include http://faketrumptweet.com, https://tweeterino.com, and http://tweetfake.com. There are also fake Facebook status generators (www.prankmenot.com/?facebook_status) and fake web page generators (www.twerkerapp.com). All of these sites rely on visual familiarity and emphasize the need for strong visual literacy skills.

Check the source: "Did Maxine Waters Blame the London Attack on Climate and Health Care 'Inaction'?" www.snopes.com/maxine-waters-london-attack-climate-healthcare/?utm_source=facebook&utm_medium=social

True or False? Fish Swim in the Streets of Miami at High Tide

True. Despite being seemingly unbelievable, this headline is true, and indicative of ongoing severe weather conditions in Miami. Because Miami is very near water, high tides and eroding shorelines enable fish and other water-based wildlife to travel inland. This phenomenon is quite well documented and photographed.

Check the source:

- "Do the Fish Swim in the Streets of Miami at High Tide, as Barack Obama Said in Paris?" www.politifact.com/florida/statements/2015/dec/04/barack-obama/do-fish-swim-streets-miami-high-tide-barack-obama-
- "During Autumn King Tides, Nuisance Flooding Becomes Chronic Flooding in Miami Area," https://www.washingtonpost.com/news/capital-weather-gang/wp/2015/10/20/during-autumn-king-tides-nuisance-flooding-becomes-chronic-flooding-in-miami-area/?utm_term=.933e29ab2309
- "South Florida's Rising Seas—Sea Level Rise Documentary," https://www.youtube.com/watch?v=-JbzypWJk64
- "Is Miami Beach Doomed?" https://www.theatlantic.com/video/index/460332/is-miami-beach-doomed

Consider the same questions that opened this report; now that you have gained some new and additional knowledge about the fake news phenomenon, have your answers changed?

- Why do these headlines ring true or false?
- If you saw these headlines on social media, would you share them with your networks?
- How would you present and explain these examples to others? What strategies and resources would you suggest?

MOVING PAST FAKE NEWS

For information professionals, particularly for those who have taught in any capacity, evaluating websites and information is not new, and the tips and tricks given below will be familiar. However, they bear repeating, as we prepare for our expanded roles as truth workers. Along with metaliteracy, these strategies should be incorporated into a larger mindset and incorporated into a larger repertoire of skills that will be used to evaluate *all* types of information, not just fake news.

Triangulate

- When you see a headline or caption about a news item, especially on social media, can you verify it with at least two other sources? Chances are that if you can't verify or find the information in another location, the information is false.

Check your own biases

- Are you assuming the information is true or false on the basis of your personal beliefs and leanings?

Read outside your bubble

- If you are a *New York Times* devotee, do you read *Breitbart News* (and vice versa)? You may not agree with what you read in other sources, but it can be helpful to be aware of the wide range of opinions that exist outside of your inner circle.

Know the difference between satire, propaganda, infotainment, opinion, and dog-whistling

- They are all related, but there are nuances between them. Knowing these distinctions will help you evaluate information.

Check Snopes, Politifact, FactCheck.org, Know Your Meme, and other fact-checking sources

- Again, can you triangulate the information you're reading/seeing?

Check the headline

- Is the headline in ALL CAPS? Is the language extreme, absurd, absolute, or flowery?

Check the source

- Is this a source you're familiar with? Is there an author? Do you know them?

What's their angle?

- Is this source considered conservative, liberal, or in between? Is what you're reading an advertisement or otherwise sponsored content?

Does the website have an "about" page?

Is the site overrun with ads?

Are there supporting sources or citations?

Check the date

- Is this news current? Or is the site appropriating old news to further a point or agenda?

Evaluating information, especially online information, and being a savvy information consumer encompasses many kinds of literacy—information, media, visual, digital, and so on. Identifying fake tweets and social media statuses (e.g., FakeTrumpTweet.com and http://simitator.com/generator/facebook), spotting photoshopped images, recognizing the underlying content in a meme (e.g., http://knowyourmeme.com), and the like require the implementation of a variety of literacy-based skills. This speaks to the advantage of assuming a metaliteracy approach to addressing fake news, and becoming critically literate in a broader sense.

LESSON PLAN

Now that you've learned more about the context of fake news, it's time to plan a lesson or workshop that will educate others. Instead of detailing a prescriptive lesson plan, this section presents a "recipe" of sorts that will allow information professionals in all settings to devise a plan that is customizable to specific settings and age levels. As an example, I will describe a workshop that was delivered to college students and adult communities at the School of Information Sciences, at the University of Illinois. The main components of the workshop are:

1. An opening activity
   - What is fake news? Why does it matter? How does it affect you as an information consumer and informed citizen?

2. Content and context
   - Definitions of terms; that is, "propaganda," "disinformation," "filter bubbles," and so on
   - What role do journalists play in fake news?
   - How does the current climate influence the creation and dissemination of fake news?
   - Why should we try to be aware of confirmation bias, filter bubbles, and other dimensions of information acquisition and sharing?
   - What is metaliteracy and why is it important?

3. Examples of fake news (as many as are appropriate and in any combination)
   - Print
   - Social media
   - Photographs
   - Videos

4. Tips, tricks, and strategies
   - Present concrete strategies for strengthening literacy skills
   - Present concrete strategies for evaluating information
   - Provide handouts or other takeaway information for future reference that includes a summary of what was covered in points 1–3.

5. Strategies in action/hands-on learning
   - Have learners search for examples of fake news/disinformation (in print or online)

     Can this information be verified?

     How can you tell if it's fake news?

   - Provide learners with pre-prepared examples of fake news and real news items

     What's fake and what's real? How do you know? What steps brought you to this conclusion?

EXAMPLES FROM THE ILLINOIS WORKSHOP

1. As an opening activity, learners participate in a quiz, such as this one produced by the BBC: www.bbc.com/news/magazine-38005844. An alternative would be to present the headlines introduced in chapter 1 of this report. Some of the items are true news items, others are not; the learners' answers should be based on their gut reactions

and do not need to be "correct." The goal is to get the audience warmed up and prepared for the discussion.

2. Learners are then presented with a brief lecture (a condensed version of chapters 1–4) where they are introduced to important terms and context related to fake news.

3. Several quick and visual examples are presented, such as a screen capture from FakeTrumpTweet.com, a photoshopped image, and the hoax site https://www.martinlutherking.org. Elements that indicate disinformation are clearly explicated. As a substantive or main example used to generate discussion, the case of the "Love Among the Ruins: The Vancouver Kiss Couple"[1] was presented. Beginning with a picture of the couple (do a quick Google images search), learners are asked to discuss what they see in the picture. Then they are presented with information from these sources (in a handout or projected on a screen):

   - http://youthandmedia.org/teaching-and-outreach/workshops/ information-quality-news-literacy/lamp-camp
   - https://thelede.blogs.nytimes.com/2011/06/24/overlooked-vancouver -video-shows-kissing-couple-was-knocked-down-by-riot-police
   - http://dlrp.berkman.harvard.edu/node/25
   - They are also shown this video: https://www.youtube.com/ watch?v=RlzNQFcUQVU and are shown additional still photographs of the couple, taken from different angles.

4. The tips and strategies for "Moving Past Fake News" that were presented earlier in this chapter are discussed with learners.

A Pinterest site was created to supplement this report and to facilitate lesson/workshop planning; the site contains hundreds of bookmarks to articles, lesson plans, videos, and other information related to the fake news phenomenon. It can be found here: https:// www.pinterest.com/nicolecooke/fake-news-alternative-facts-critical-literacy.

NOTE

1. Everyone is a consumer of information, and everyone should have the skills necessary to be critical consumers and creators of information. Becoming metaliterate in a way that is especially effective in the online domain takes practice and diligence, and begins with learning in the classroom and in libraries. The end goal is to produce proactive critical thinkers, researchers, and information consumers who can sidestep false information and its deleterious effects. Special thanks to Dr. Rachel Magee (School of Information Sciences, University of Illinois) for suggesting "Love Among the Ruins" as an example.

In February 2017, I presented a webinar for the American Library Association on the topic of fake news; it was this webinar that inspired this report. A recording of the webinar is referenced here:

Cooke, N. A. "Post-Truth: Fake News and a New Era of Information Literacy." *Programming Librarian: A Website of the American Library Association Public Programs Office.* February 2017. (Invited webinar). http://programminglibrarian.org/learn/post-truth-fake-news-and-new -era-information-literacy.

A Pinterest site was created to supplement this webinar; the site contains hundreds of bookmarks to articles, lesson plans, videos, and other information related to the fake news phenomenon. It can be found here: https://www.pinterest.com/nicolecooke/fake -news-alternative-facts-critical-literacy.

THE LARGER CONTEXT OF FAKE NEWS—SUGGESTED BOOKS

Booth, Char. *Reflective Teaching, Effective Learning: Instructional Literacy for Library Educators.* American Library Association, 2011.

Boyd, Danah. *It's Complicated: The Social Lives of Networked Teens.* Yale University Press, 2014.

Carr, Nicholas. *The Shallows: What the Internet Is Doing to Our Brains.* W. W. Norton, 2011.

Kovach, Bill, and Tom Rosenstiel. *Blur: How to Know What's True in the Age of Information Overload.* Bloomsbury Publishing USA, 2011.

Levitin, Daniel J. *A Field Guide to Lies: Critical Thinking in the Information Age.* Penguin, 2016.

———. *The Organized Mind: Thinking Straight in the Age of Information Overload.* Penguin, 2014.

Pariser, Eli. *The Filter Bubble: What the Internet Is Hiding from You.* Penguin UK, 2011.

Sloman, Steven, and Philip Fernbach. *The Knowledge Illusion: Why We Never Think Alone.* Penguin, 2017.

Stanley, Jason. *How Propaganda Works.* Princeton University Press, 2015.

MULTIPLE FORMS OF LITERACY—
SUGGESTED ARTICLES AND WEBSITES

Area, Manuel, and Teresa Pessoa. "From Solid to Liquid: New Literacies to the Cultural Changes of Web 2.0." *Comunicar* 38, no. 19 (2012): 13–20.

Buschman, John. "Information Literacy, 'New' Literacies, and Literacy." *The Library Quarterly* 79, no. 1 (2009): 95–118.

Cooke, Nicole A. "Becoming an Andragogical Librarian: Using Library Instruction as a Tool to Combat Library Anxiety and Empower Adult Learners." *New Review of Academic Librarianship* 16, no. 2 (2010): 208–27.

Cope, Bill, and Mary Kalantzis. "'Multiliteracies': New Literacies, New Learning." *Pedagogies: An International Journal* 4, no. 3 (2009): 164–95.

Dunaway, Michelle Kathleen. "Connectivism: Learning Theory and Pedagogical Practice for Networked Information Landscapes." *Reference Services Review* 39, no. 4 (2011): 675–85.

Eisenberg, Michael B., Carrie A. Lowe, and Kathleen L. Spitzer. *Information Literacy: Essential Skills for the Information Age.* Westport, CT: Greenwood, 2004.

Grassian, Esther. "Information Literacy and Instruction: Teaching and Learning Alternatives: A Global Overview." *Reference & User Services Quarterly* 56, no. 4 (2017): 232–39.

Harris, Benjamin R. "Blurring Borders, Visualizing Connections: Aligning Information and Visual Literacy Learning Outcomes." *Reference Services Review* 38, no. 4 (2010): 523–35.

Hattwig, Denise, Kaila Bussert, Ann Medaille, and Joanna Burgess. "Visual Literacy Standards in Higher Education: New Opportunities for Libraries and Student Learning." *portal: Libraries and the Academy* 13, no. 1 (2013): 61–89.

Head, Alison, et al. "Project Information Literacy." www.projectinfolit.org.

Higgins, Shana, and Lua Gregory. *Information Literacy and Social Justice: Radical Professional Praxis.* Library Juice, 2013.

Ipri, Thomas A. "Introducing Transliteracy: What Does It Mean to Academic Libraries?" *College and Research Libraries News* 71, no. 10 (2010): 532–33, 567.

Jacobs, Heidi L. M. "Information Literacy and Reflective Pedagogical Praxis." *The Journal of Academic Librarianship* 34, no. 3 (2008): 256–62.

Koltay, Tibor. "The Media and the Literacies: Media Literacy, Information Literacy, Digital Literacy." *Media, Culture & Society* 33, no. 2 (2011): 211–21.

Limberg, Louise, Mikael Alexandersson, Annika Lantz-Andersson, and Lena Folkesson. "What Matters? Shaping Meaningful Learning through Teaching Information Literacy." *Libri* 58, no. 2 (2008): 82–91.

Limberg, Louise, Olof Sundin, and Sanna Talja. "Three Theoretical Perspectives on Information Literacy." *Human IT: Journal for Information Technology Studies as a Human Science* 11, no. 2 (2013): 93–130.

Lloyd, Annemaree. "Information Literacy Landscapes: An Emerging Picture." *Journal of Documentation* 62, no. 5 (2006): 570–83.

————. "Information Literacy: Different Contexts, Different Concepts, Different Truths?" *Journal of Librarianship and Information Science* 37, no. 2 (2005): 82–88.

————. "Information Literacy: The Meta-Competency of the Knowledge Economy? An Exploratory Paper." *Journal of Librarianship and Information Science* 35, no. 2 (2003): 87–92.

Marcum, James W. "Rethinking Information Literacy." *The Library Quarterly* 72, no. 1 (2002): 1–26.

Matteson, Miriam L. "The Whole Student: Cognition, Emotion, and Information Literacy." *College and Research Libraries* 75, no. 6 (2014): 862.

Nelson, Nerissa. "Visual Literacy and Library Instruction: A Critical Analysis." *Education Libraries* 27, no. 1 (2004): 5–10.

New London Group. "A Pedagogy of Multiliteracies: Designing Social Futures." *Harvard Educational Review* 66, no. 1 (1996): 60–93.

Owusu-Ansah, Edward K. "Information Literacy and the Academic Library: A Critical Look at a Concept and the Controversies Surrounding It." *The Journal of Academic Librarianship* 29, no. 4 (2003): 219–30.

Pinto, Maria, Jose Antonio Cordon, and Raquel Gómez Díaz. "Thirty Years of Information Literacy (1977–2007): A Terminological, Conceptual and Statistical Analysis." *Journal of Librarianship and Information Science* 42, no. 1 (2010): 3–19.

Rader, Hannelore B. "Information Literacy 1973–2002: A Selected Literature Review." *Library Trends* 51, no. 2 (2002): 242–59.

Rheingold, Howard. "Stewards of Digital Literacies." *Knowledge Quest* 41, no. 1 (2012): 53–55.

Snavely, Loanne, and Natasha Cooper. "The Information Literacy Debate." *The Journal of Academic Librarianship* 23, no. 1 (1997): 9–14.

Swanson, Troy A. "A Radical Step: Implementing a Critical Information Literacy Model." *portal: Libraries and the Academy* 4, no. 2 (2004): 259–73.

Tewell, Eamon. "A Decade of Critical Information Literacy: A Review of the Literature." *Communications in Information Literacy* 9, no. 1 (2015): 24–43.

Thomas, Sue, Chris Joseph, Jess Laccetti, Bruce Mason, Simon Mills, Simon Perril, and Kate Pullinger. "Transliteracy: Crossing Divides." *First Monday* 12, no. 12 (2007). www.ojphi.org/ojs/index.php/fm/article/view/2060.

Tripp, Lisa. "Digital Youth, Libraries, and New Media Literacy." *The Reference Librarian* 52, no. 4 (2011): 329–41.

RESOURCES FOR INFORMATION CONSUMERS

Fact-Checking

Snopes: www.snopes.com/info/aboutus.asp

The snopes.com website was founded by David Mikkelson, who lives and works in the Los Angeles area. What he began in 1995 as an expression of his interest in researching urban legends has since grown into what is widely regarded by folklorists, journalists, and laypersons alike as one of the Web's essential resources. Snopes.com is routinely included in annual "Best of the Web" lists and has been the recipient of two Webby awards. The Mikkelsons have made multiple appearances as guests on national news programs such as *20/20, ABC World News, CNN Sunday Morning*, and NPR's *All Things Considered*. They and their work have been profiled in numerous major news publications, including the *New York Times, Los Angeles Times, Washington Post, Wall Street Journal*, and an April 2009 *Reader's Digest* feature ("The Rumor Detectives") published as part of that magazine's "Your America: Inspiring People and Stories" series.

PolitiFact: www.politifact.com

PolitiFact is a fact-checking website that rates the accuracy of claims by elected officials and others who speak up in American politics. PolitiFact is run by editors and reporters from the *Tampa Bay Times*, an independent newspaper in Florida, as is PunditFact, a site devoted to fact-checking pundits. The PolitiFact state sites are run by news organizations that have partnered with the *Times*. The state sites and PunditFact follow the same principles as the national site.

checkology® Virtual Classroom:
www.thenewsliteracyproject.org/services/checkology

The News Literacy Project's checkology® virtual classroom is an innovative space where students discover how to effectively navigate today›s challenging information landscape by mastering the core skills and concepts of news literacy.

It equips students with the tools to interpret the news and information that shape their lives so they can make informed decisions about what to believe, share, and act on—and ultimately become active members of civic society.

The Fact Checker (The Washington Post):
https://www.washingtonpost.com/news/fact-checker

This column first started on September 19, 2007, as a feature during the 2008 presidential campaign. The *Washington Post* revived it as a permanent feature on January 11, 2011. The purpose of this website, and an accompanying column in the Sunday print edition of the *Washington Post*, is to "truth squad" the statements of political figures regarding issues of great importance, be they national, international or local. But it is not limited to political charges or countercharges. It also seeks to explain difficult issues, provide missing context, and provide analysis and explanation of various "code words" used by politicians, diplomats, and others to obscure or shade the truth.

FactCheck.org: https://www.factcheck.org

FactCheck is a nonpartisan, nonprofit "consumer advocate" for voters that aims to reduce the level of deception and confusion in U.S. politics. It monitors the factual accuracy of what is said by major U.S. political players in the form of TV ads, debates, speeches, interviews, and news releases. Their goal is to apply the best practices of both journalism and scholarship, and to increase public knowledge and understanding.

FactCheck.org is a project of the Annenberg Public Policy Center of the University of Pennsylvania. The APPC was established by publisher and philanthropist Walter Annenberg to create a community of scholars within the University of Pennsylvania that would address public policy issues at the local, state, and federal levels.

Graphics

HOW TO SPOT FAKE NEWS

CONSIDER THE SOURCE

Click away from the story to investigate the site, its mission and its contact info.

READ BEYOND

Headlines can be outrageous in an effort to get clicks. What's the whole story?

CHECK THE AUTHOR

Do a quick search on the author. Are they credible? Are they real?

SUPPORTING SOURCES?

Click on those links. Determine if the info given actually supports the story.

CHECK THE DATE

Reposting old news stories doesn't mean they're relevant to current events.

IS IT A JOKE?

If it is too outlandish, it might be satire. Research the site and author to be sure.

CHECK YOUR BIASES

Consider if your own beliefs could affect your judgement.

ASK THE EXPERTS

Ask a librarian, or consult a fact-checking site.

IFLA
International Federation of Library Associations and Institutions
With thanks to www.FactCheck.org

Figure 1. How to Spot Fake News

¿ESTA NOTICIA ES FALSA?

ESTUDIE LA FUENTE
Investigue más allá: el sitio web, objetivo e información de contacto.

LEA MÁS ALLÁ
Un titular impactante puede querer captar su atención. ¿Cuál es la historia completa?

¿QUIÉN ES EL AUTOR?
Haga una búsqueda rápida sobre el autor. ¿Es fiable? ¿Es real?

FUENTES ADICIONALES
Haga clic en los enlaces y compruebe que haya datos que avalen la información.

COMPRUEBE LA FECHA
Publicar viejas noticias no significa que sean relevantes para hechos actuales.

¿ES UNA BROMA?
Si es muy extravagante puede ser una sátira. Investigue el sitio web y el autor.

CONSIDERE SU SESGO
Tenga en cuenta que sus creencias podrían alterar su opinión.

PREGUNTE AL EXPERTO
Consulte a un bibliotecario o un sitio web de verificación.

Traducido por Diego Gracia

IFLA
International Federation of Library Associations and Institutions
Agradecimientos a www.FactCheck.org

Figure 2. ¿Esta Noticia Es Falsa?

✂ CUT OUT AND TAPE NEAR YOUR COMPUTER OR TV

[BREAKING NEWS CONSUMER'S HANDBOOK]

FAKE NEWS EDITION

1. Big red flags for fake news: ALL CAPS, or obviously photoshopped pics.

2. A glut of pop-ups and banner ads? Good sign the story is pure clickbait.

3. Check the domain! Fake sites often add ".co" to trusted brands to steal their luster. (Think: "abcnews.com.co")

4. If you land on an unknown site, check its "About" page. Then, Google it with the word "fake" and see what comes up.

5. If a story offers links, follow them. (Garbage leads to worse garbage.) No links, quotes, or references? Another telltale sign.

6. Verify an unlikely story by finding a reputable outlet reporting the same thing.

7. Check the date. Social media often resurrects outdated stories.

8. Read past headlines. Often they bear no resemblance to what lies beneath.

9. Photos may be misidentified and dated. Use a reverse image search engine like TinEye to see where an image *really* comes from.

10. Gut check. If a story makes you angry, it's probably designed that way.

11. Finally, if you're not sure it's true, don't share it! *Don't. Share. It.*

ON [THE MEDIA]   ONTHEMEDIA.ORG

Figure 3. Breaking News Consumer's Handbook: Fake News Edition
Courtesy of On The Media from WNYC Studios.
Retrieved from https://www.wnyc.org/story/breaking-news-consumer-handbook-fake-news-edition.

Don't Get Fooled: 7 Simple Steps

the
news
literacy
project

Use the steps and questions below to avoid being manipulated, fooled or exploited by viral rumors, misleading memes, imposter news sites and fake images.

1. CHECK YOUR EMOTIONS: WHAT'S YOUR FIRST REACTION?

- **Are you angry? Outraged? Curious? Excited?**
  Misinformation often tries to hijack our rational minds with emotional appeals.

2. DETERMINE THE PURPOSE OF WHAT YOU'RE READING, WATCHING OR HEARING:

- **Is it a news report? An opinion column? An ad? Satire?**
  Knowing what it is helps you decide whether to trust it.
- **What do you know about the source (news outlet, blog, video producer, etc.)?**
  Does it have an "About Us" (or similar) page? Does it provide biographical or contact information for its employees and contributors?

3. BE AWARE OF YOUR BIASES:

- **Are you assuming — or hoping — that it's true? Or that it's false?**
  You're more likely to be less critical of information that "feels" right.

4. CONSIDER THE MESSAGE:

- Is it "too perfect"?
- Is it overtly or aggressively partisan?
- Does it use loaded language, excessive punctuation — !!!— Or ALL CAPS for emphasis?
- Does it claim to contain a secret or tell you something that "the media" doesn't want you to know?

5. SEARCH FOR MORE INFORMATION:

- Are reputable news outlets reporting the same thing?
- Have independent fact-checkers contested or debunked it?
- Can you determine where it first appeared?

6. GO DEEPER ON THE SOURCE:

- Search for its name, then do a <u>WHOIS search</u> on its web domain. What do you find?
- Does it use social media responsibly? Do its posts and tweets appear reliable?
- Does it promptly correct errors in a transparent manner?
  Does the site include silly bylines or section headings?
  Are there disclaimers anywhere on the site labeling it as satirical or fictional?

7. THEN GO DEEPER ON THE CONTENT ITSELF:

- Search the byline: Is it a real person or a made-up name?
- Is what is being reported old or outdated information?
- Can you confirm key details (date, time, location)?
- Search any quotes used: Are they accurate? Are they presented in context?
- Do a reverse image search on photos and graphics: Do they appear elsewhere online?
  If so, are they shown in a different context? Have they been altered?

REMEMBER:

Visual misinformation is compelling.
People instinctively trust images more than words. Misinformation peddlers often try to use this against you.

Convincing fakes are easy to make.
Digital tools, such as Photoshop, and "create a fake" websites enable anyone to manipulate or falsify just about anything — social media posts, news reports, images and videos.

Bots and trolls are all over social media.
Not every account represents a person, and not all people express what they really think.

Information is the basis for decisions and actions.
Even if you're not fooled by a piece of misinformation, someone else whose decisions affect others may be. Help debunk examples of misinformation whenever you see them!

<u>www.thenewsliteracyproject.org</u>

Figure 4. Don't Get Fooled: 7 Simple Steps
Courtesy of the News Literacy Project.

Protect Yourself from
Fake News

Nine Tips to Help You Separate Fact from Fiction

Be Skeptical

Does the headline sound unlikely, unrealistic, preposterous? Don't take every headline you see at face value.

Identify the Author

Many fake news stories are anonymous. If you can't find out who wrote the information, be wary of the content.

Spell Check

Does the url have any odd suffixes or substitutions (like replacing a letter l with a numeral 1, for example)? Is this a fake news site pretending to be something else?

Compare and Contrast

Compare the headline and/or picture against the content of the article. If they don't match, are they meant to mislead or misdirect you?

Consult Multiple Sources

Check other sources. Are they reporting the same or similar news? If it's a big story, they will. What do "opposition" sources say about the story? Do they report the same facts?

Check It Out

Fact check the story with watch dog sites such as Snopes.com, Politico.com, and PolitiFact.com. They make it their job to make sure the information from news sites is accurate.

Dig Deeper

Does the article cite sources or traceable quotes? Find and read the actual study for confirmation. Put quotes in context.

Beware Online "Filter Bubbles"

Is predictive searching biasing your information retrieval? Social media often feeds you only items that are similar to items you have liked. This keeps you from getting both "sides" of a story.

Be Open-Minded

Is confirmation bias—the tendency to believe reports that confirm what you already believe—putting you in an echo chamber? Be open-minded. Ask questions.

Figure 5. Fact or Fiction

REFERENCES

ABC News. 2017 (June 27). "Hillary Clinton Live Remarks: Keynote Address at ALA Conference and Exhibition in Chicago" (video file). https://www.youtube.com/watch?v=2bDQIP45OuY&feature=youtu.be.

Abercrombie, Nicholas, and Brian J. Longhurst. 1998. *Audiences: A Sociological Theory of Performance and Imagination.* Thousand Oaks, CA: Sage.

Accardi, Maria T., Emily E. Drabinski, and Alana A. Kumbier, eds. 2010. *Critical Library Instruction: Theories and Methods.* Sacramento, CA: Library Juice.

Area, Manuel, and Teresa Pessoa. 2012. "From Solid to Liquid: New Literacies to the Cultural Changes of Web 2.0." *Comunicar* 38, no. 19: 13–20.

Attkisson, Sharyl. 2017 (April 23). "Media Bias: A New Chart." https://sharylattkisson.com/media-bias-a-new-chart.

Badke, William B. 2015. "Expertise and Authority in an Age of Crowdsourcing." In *Not Just Where to Click: Teaching Students How to Think about Information,* 191–216. Chicago: Association of College and Research Libraries.

Bawden, David. 2008. "Origins and Concepts of Digital Literacy." In *Digital Literacies: Concepts, Policies and Practices,* 17–32. Peter Lang, 2008.

Bawden, David, and Lyn Robinson. 2002. "Promoting Literacy in a Digital Age: Approaches to Training for Information Literacy." *Learned Publishing* 15, no. 4: 297–301.

Booth, Char. 2011. *Reflective Teaching, Effective Learning: Instructional Literacy for Library Educators.* Chicago: American Library Association.

Borchers, Callum. 2017 (July 7). "Rachel Maddow's Urgent Warning to the Rest of the Media." https://www.washingtonpost.com/news/the-fix/wp/2017/07/07/rachel-maddows-urgent-warning-to-the-rest-of-the-media/?utm_term=.fed30b357397.

Buckingham, David. 2013. *Media Education: Literacy, Learning and Contemporary Culture.* John Wiley & Sons.

Calamur, Krishnadev. 2015 (June 18). "It's Official: Brian Williams Out as 'NBC Nightly News' Anchor." The Two-Way: Breaking News from NPR (web log). www.npr.org/sections/thetwo-way/2015/06/18/415519389/its-official-brian-williams-out-as-nbc-nightly-news-anchor.

Case, Donald O., and Lisa M. Given, eds. 2016. *Looking for Information: A Survey of Research on Information Seeking, Needs, and Behavior.* Bingley, UK: Emerald Group.

Cohen, Daniel. 2000. *Yellow Journalism: Scandal, Sensationalism, and Gossip in the Media.* Millbrook.

Colbert, Stephen. 2005 (October 17). "Truthiness." *The Colbert Report*. Comedy Central.
    www.cc.com/video-clips/63ite2/the-colbert-report-the-word---truthiness.

Columbia Journalism Review. 2017. "Who Owns What?" http://archives.cjr.org/
    resources/?c=comcast.

Cooper, Anderson (producer). 2017 (April 7). "Why Can't We Put Down Our Smartphones?"
    (television series episode). *60 Minutes*. New York: CBS.

Cope, Bill, and Mary Kalantzis. 2009. "'Multiliteracies': New Literacies, New Learning."
    Pedagogies: An International Journal 4, no. 3: 164–95.

Craft, Stephanie, and Charles N. Davis. 2016. *Principles of American Journalism: An Introduction*.
    Routledge.

De Abreu, B. 2010. "Changing Technology = Empowering Students through Media Literacy
    Education." *New Horizons in Education* 58, no. 3: 26–33.

De Saulles, Martin. *Information 2.0: New Models of Information Production, Distribution and
    Consumption*. Facet, 2015.

Dictionary.com, s.v. "tldr." www.dictionary.com/browse/tldr.

Eisenberg, Michael B., Carrie A. Lowe, and Kathleen L. Spitzer. 2004. *Information Literacy:
    Essential Skills for the Information Age*. Westport, CT: Greenwood.

Elmborg, James. 2006. "Critical Information Literacy: Implications for Instructional Practice."
    The Journal of Academic Librarianship 32, no. 2: 192–99.

Fallis, Don. 2009 (February 28). "A Conceptual Analysis of Disinformation." Presented at the
    fourth annual iConference ("iSociety: Research, Education, Engagement") sponsored by the
    iSchools Caucus, University of North Carolina–Chapel Hill. https://www.ideals.illinois.edu/
    handle/2142/15201/browse.

Fox, Christopher J. 1983. *Information and Misinformation: An Investigation of the Notions of
    Information, Misinformation, Informing, and Misinforming*. Westport, CT: Greenwood.

Gil, Paul. 2016 (October 26). "What Is 'TLDR'?" Lifewire. https://www.lifewire.com.

Gilster, Paul. 1997. *Digital Literacy*. New York: Wiley Computer Publications.

Head, Alison, and John Wihbey. 2017 (April 8). "The Importance of Truth Workers in an Era of
    Factual Recession" (web log post). https://medium.com/@ajhead1/the-importance-of-truth
    -workers-in-an-era-of-factual-recession-7487fda8eb3b.

Hernon, Peter. 1995. "Disinformation and Misinformation through the Internet: Findings of an
    Exploratory Study." *Government Information Quarterly* 12, no. 2: 133–39.

Hobbs, R. 2011. "The State of Media Literacy: A Response to Potter." *Journal of Broadcasting &
    Electronic Media* 55, no. 3: 419–30.

Holiday, Ryan. 2013. *Trust Me, I'm Lying: Confessions of a Media Manipulator*. Penguin.

hooks, bell. 2010. *Teaching Critical Thinking: Practical Wisdom*. Routledge.

Illeris, K. 2002. *The Three Dimensions of Learning: Contemporary Theory in the Tension Field between
    the Cognitive, Emotional, and Social*. Frederiksberg: Roskilde University Press.

Jackson, Brooks, and Kathleen Hall Jamieson. 2007. *UnSpun: Finding Facts in a World of Disinformation*. Random House.

Jacobson, Trudi E., and Thomas P. Mackey, eds. 2016. *Metaliteracy in Practice*. American Library Association.

Jacobson, Trudi E., and Thomas P. Mackey. 2013. "Proposing a Metaliteracy Model to Redefine Information Literacy." *Communications in Information Literacy* 7, no. 2: 84–91.

Jerz, Dennis G. 2016 (December 12). "Vanessa Otero's Complex vs. Clickbait, Liberal vs. Conservative Media Chart." https://jerz.setonhill.edu/blog/2016/12/12/vanessa-oteros-media-complexclickbait-liberalconservative-chart.

Karlova, Natascha, and Jin Ha Lee. 2011. "Notes from the Underground City of Disinformation: A Conceptual Investigation." *Proceedings of the American Society for Information Science and Technology* 48, no. 1: 1–9.

Kovach, Bill, and Tom Rosenstiel. 2011. *Blur: How to Know What's True in the Age of Information Overload*. Bloomsbury Publishing USA.

Kuhlthau, Carol C. 1987. *Information Skills for an Information Society* (Report ED 297740). Syracuse, NY: ERIC Clearinghouse on Educational Resources.

Lanham, Richard A. 1995. "Digital Literacy." *Scientific American* 273, no. 3: 160–61.

Lankshear, Colin, and Michele Knobel. 2011. *New Literacies*. McGraw-Hill Education UK.

Le, Vanna. 2015 (May 22). "The World's Largest Media Companies of 2015." https://www.forbes.com/sites/vannale/2015/05/22/the-worlds-largest-media-companies-of-2015/#3656538b4161.

Levitin, Daniel J. 2016. *A Field Guide to Lies: Critical Thinking in the Information Age*. Penguin.

Losee, Robert M. 1997. "A Discipline-Independent Definition of Information." *Journal of the American Society for Information Science* 48, no. 3: 254–69.

Mackey, Thomas P., and Trudi E. Jacobson. 2011. "Reframing Information Literacy as a Metaliteracy." *College & Research Libraries* 76, no. 1: 62–78.

———. 2014. *Metaliteracy: Reinventing Information Literacy to Empower Learners*. Chicago: American Library Association.

Miller, Willie. 2015. "Fragmented Stories: Uncovering News Bias through Information Literacy Instruction." In *Not Just Where to Click: Teaching Students How to Think about Information*, 311–25. Chicago: Association of College and Research Libraries.

NBC News. 2017 (January 22). "Conway: Press Secretary Gave 'Alternative Facts'" (video file). https://www.nbcnews.com/meet-the-press/video/conway-press-secretary-gave-alternative-facts-860142147643.

New London Group. 1996. "A Pedagogy of Multiliteracies: Designing Social Futures." *Harvard Educational Review* 66, no. 1: 60–93.

Pew Research. 2017 (June 16). "Media Ownership." www.pewresearch.org/topics/media-ownership/.

Rosen, Jay. 2017 (February 6). "The Last Word with Lawrence O'Donnell. Transcript." MSNBC. www.msnbc.com/transcripts/the-last-word/2017–02–06.

Rubin, Victoria L. 2010. "On Deception and Deception Detection: Content Analysis of Computer-Mediated Stated Beliefs." *Proceedings of the American Society for Information Science and Technology* 47, no. 1: 1–10.

Selyukh, Alina, Maria Hollenhorst, and Katie Park. 2016 (October 28). "Big Media Companies and Their Many Brands—in One Chart." www.npr.org/sections/alltechconsidered/2016/10/28/499495517/big-media-companies-and-their-many-brands-in-one-chart.

Shane, S., and V. Goel. 2017, September 6. "Fake Russian Facebook Accounts Bought $100,000 in Political Ads." *New York Times,* 6.

Stanley, Jason. 2015. *How Propaganda Works.* Princeton University Press.

Tisdell, Elizabeth J. 2008. "Critical Media Literacy and Transformative Learning: Drawing on Pop Culture and Entertainment Media in Teaching for Diversity in Adult Higher Education." *Journal of Transformative Education* 6, no. 1: 48–67.

Vinton, Kate. 2016 (June 2). "These 15 Billionaires Own America's News Media Companies." https://www.forbes.com/sites/katevinton/2016/06/01/these-15-billionaires-own-americas-news-media-companies/#22b86c94660a.

Walczyk, Jeffrey J., Mark A. Runco, Sunny M. Tripp, and Christian E. Smith. 2008. "The Creativity of Lying: Divergent Thinking and Ideational Correlates of the Resolution of Social Dilemmas." *Creativity Research Journal* 20, no. 3: 328–42.

Walsh, John. 2010. "Librarians and Controlling Disinformation: Is Multi-Literacy Instruction the Answer?" *Library Review* 59, no. 7: 498–511.

Witek, Donna, and Teresa Grettano. 2014. "Teaching Metaliteracy: A New Paradigm in Action." *Reference Services Review* 42, no. 2: 188–208.

Zhou, Lina, and Dongsong Zhang. 2007. "An Ontology-Supported Misinformation Model: Toward a Digital Misinformation Library." *Systems, Man and Cybernetics,* Part A: Systems and Humans, IEEE Transactions 37, no. 5: 804–13.

ABOUT THE AUTHOR

DR. NICOLE A. COOKE is an assistant professor at the School of Information Sciences of the University of Illinois, Urbana-Champaign, where she is also the program director for the Masters of Library and Information Science program. Cooke received a PhD degree in communication, information, and library studies from Rutgers University in 2012, where she was one of the first 12 American Library Association Spectrum Doctoral Fellows. She holds an MLS degree from Rutgers University, and an M.Ed. in adult education from Pennsylvania State University. Previously, she was a tenured reference and instruction librarian at Montclair State University (NJ).

Cooke is professionally active in the ALA, the Association of College and Research Libraries, the Association of Library and Information Science Educators (ALISE), and several other professional library organizations. She was awarded the 2017 ALA Achievement in Library Diversity Research Award, presented by the ALA's Office for Diversity and Literacy Outreach Services, and she received the 2016 ALA Equality Award. She has also been honored as the University of Illinois YWCA's 2015 Leadership Award in Education winner in recognition of her work in social justice and higher education, and she was selected as the university's 2016 Larine Y. Cowan Make a Difference Award for Teaching and Mentoring in Diversity. She was the 2013 Recipient of the Norman Horrocks Leadership Award given by ALISE, and *Library Journal* named her a Mover & Shaker in 2007.

Cooke's research and teaching interests include human information behavior (particularly in the online context), critical cultural information studies, and diversity and social justice in librarianship (with an emphasis on infusing them into LIS education and pedagogy). She has published articles in journals including *The Library Quarterly, Library & Information Science Research, Libraries: Culture, History, and Society, InterActions: UCLA Journal of Education and Information, Journal of the Association for Information Science and Technology, Online Learning* (the official journal of the Online Learning Consortium). *Polymath: An Interdisciplinary Arts and Sciences Journal, Information Research, The Journal of Library & Information Services in Distance Learning, The New Review of Academic Librarianship,* and *The Library and Book Trade Almanac 2013.* Cooke coauthored *Instructional Strategies and Techniques for Information Professionals* (Chandos Press, 2012), and co-edited *Teaching for Justice: Implementing Social Justice in the LIS Classroom* (Library Juice Press, 2017). Her latest work is *Information Services to Diverse Populations* (Libraries Unlimited, 2016).